FASTING & PRAYER

A SEVEN DAY JOURNEY

Nick Serb

EMPOWERED FOR MORE
series

"Every great movement of God can be traced to a kneeling figure."

D.L. Moody
(5 Feb. 1837 – 22 Dec. 1899)

THINK FASTING AND PRAYER
Copyright © 2022 by Nick Serb

ISBN: 978-1-915223-07-4

All rights reserved.
No part of this publication may be reproduced, stored in a retrieval system, or transmitted in any form or by any means, electronic, mechanical, photocopying or otherwise, without prior written consent of the publisher except as provided by under United Kingdom copyright law. Short extracts may be used for review purposes with credits given.

Unless otherwise indicated, all Scripture quotations are taken from the *Holy Bible*, New Living Translation, copyright © 1996, 2004, 2015 by Tyndale House Foundation. Used by permission of Tyndale House Publishers, Inc., Carol Stream, Illinois 60188. All rights reserved.

Scripture quotations marked Message Bible are taken from *THE MESSAGE*, copyright © 1993, 2002, 2018 by Eugene H. Peterson. Used by permission of NavPress. All rights reserved. Represented by Tyndale House Publishers, Inc.

Emphasis within Scripture quotations is the author's own.

Published by
Maurice Wylie Media
Your Inspirational Christian Publisher

Publisher's statement: Throughout this book the love for our God is such that whenever we refer to Him we honour with capitals. On the other hand, when referring to the devil, we refuse to acknowledge him with any honour to the point of violating grammatical rule and withholding capitalisation.

For more information visit
www.MauriceWylieMedia.com

Introducing the...

'Empowered for More' Series

If you ever felt helpless or inadequate as a Christian, let me say you are not on your own. Christian life is often full of difficult decisions. That is why we need to comfort one another in the fact that life as a Christian is not meant to be lived in our own strength or wisdom.

One thing I have learnt is that I cannot do anything by myself. Jesus, in fact, makes that quite clear when He said: *"For apart from me you can do nothing"* John 15:5b.

This series of books is meant to introduce you to the wonderful reality of being empowered by the Holy Spirit to do things you never thought you could do. And when you feel empowered, the Holy Spirit comes to empower you for more.

May you know and experience the power of the Holy Spirit as you journey with these books, doing the things you thought were impossible.

Endorsements

Nick's manual is a very practical guide to experience what the Danish Christian, Kierkegaard said: 'It is more blessed to give than to receive, but then it is also more blessed to be able to do without than to have.'

Desi Maxwell
Teacher and founder of Xplorations Ministries, UK.

Nick and I share a few things in common, beyond Bruce Willis hairstyles, in particular our love for family life, sports and a passion for Evangelism. In the ten years I have known Nick, he continues to be a faithful steward of all that the LORD has entrusted to him as well as a pioneer seeking fresh ways to reach lost people and multiply the mission of God. This book flows out of a deep river of theology and practice that is both relevant and challenging. I have read a few books on fasting and prayer, some are simply too 'Pentecostal' or 'too radical' for most people to grasp. They set the bar too high. Others are filled with too many personal stories and you come away talking about the author instead of Jesus or the power of fasting and prayer. This book gets the balance just right, Biblical, practical and accessible to all.

I wholeheartedly recommend this book to every Christian.

Read it, act on it, journal your experience, keep a prayer diary and wait upon the Lord. He will answer. I am convinced this book has the potential to help light a spark that can, as Nick puts it, turn us all into spiritually 'highly flammable' followers of Jesus.

Mitch
Evangelist and co-founder of Crown Jesus Ministries, UK and Ireland.

Nick's passion to see the Church revived and operating in the power of the Holy Spirit as we rediscover the joy of worshipping God in fasting and prayer is refreshing. He does this in a very practical, easy to read book which encourages us to adopt the practice of the important disciplines of fasting and prayer.

Rev. John Townley
National Leader of the Free Methodist Church, UK.

We live across the road from a tennis club. For years now, we have watched a little boy arriving early in the morning for personal coaching. He is probably about fourteen years old now. From his and his coach's body language, he clearly gets some things wrong, but they persist and he is developing into a very good player. "Practice makes perfect," so the saying goes.

I recently spoke to a member of our church who comes to our prayer meetings, but never prays. 'I'm just not good at it,' she says.

When it comes to prayer and fasting, many Christians have a great sense of failure because they think that they're "just not good at it." Reading books on the subject can often deepen that sense of failure.

Pastor Nick Serb moves beyond the theory of "books" to getting stuck in and practising prayer and fasting in clear, simple and spiritually adventurous steps. Practice makes perfect, so go on; dare to journey.

Rev. Andrew Gardner
Lead pastor, Hope Church Lancaster, England.

Fasting and prayer. Unfortunately, both are becoming less of a major part of the Christian community. It is time this book is read and this book is studied and this book is practiced. Pastor Nick takes us into the very presence of God with this study. May this book turn our hearts nearer to the heart of God.

Dr. H. Wallace Webster
Author and Pastor of Mount Airy Bible Church and Elementary, Principal of Mount Airy Christian Academy, Maryland, USA.

Readable, Biblical, practical, timely — full of devotional warmth and realism.

Dr. John M. Haley
Superintendent Minister, Torbay Methodist Circuit, England.

Almost three millennia ago, God spoke through the Prophet Hosea, "Plow up the hard ground of your hearts, for now is the time to seek the LORD, that he may come and shower righteousness upon you. (Hosea 10:12). Many hearts resonate with this message. We want to plow the hard ground in our hearts, but often don't know where to begin. Pastor Nick Serb provides some answers: prayer and fasting. Our flesh wishes there was another way; a way that avoids brokenness. But, as Pastor Nick observes, brokenness is the route to joy. We are pleased to recommend this resource to you as a tool to help you seek the Lord until He showers righteousness on you, and me, and the hurting world around us.

Dr. Ivan L. Filby
12th President, Greenville University, USA.

Fasting and Prayer is one of the most dynamic and personal books written in the area of Christian spirituality. Pastor Nick creates a perfect balance between the theological knowledge of fasting and prayer and the practical challenge of experiencing this spiritual discipline. Although our Christian theology has been enriched by many thematic writings on the subject of prayer, few books have managed the transition from theory to practice. The author uses personal experiences and writes in a very pleasant manner. I believe reading the book will revolutionise the life of any reader. I wholeheartedly recommend this book.

Dr. Radu Cimpeanu
Pastor of Bethany Baptist Church, lecturer at the Baptist Theological College Sibiu, Romania and assistant professor at the Baptist Theological Institute, Bucharest, Romania.

This book that captivated my attention from the first few pages. It made me realise how much the Christian community has been missing by forgetting the importance of fasting and prayer. The book genuinely challenged me to bring myself, my family and my church back to the life-giving practice of fasting and prayer.

Petry Groza
President and Founder of Regen Foundation, Fagaras, Romania and Vice President of Horizon of Hope, Wisconsin, USA.

Fasting seems to be rarely discussed in many churches. Either we are faithfully obeying Jesus' instruction to fast in secret, or we have, in unfaithful disobedience, turned the assumptions of His 'when you fast' into an optional 'if you fast'. For such a time as this, Nick Serb helps us rediscover this vital practice as a channel through which our worship flows to God and His grace flows to us.

Dr David A. Hull
Chair, Methodist Evangelicals Together.

Excellent, practical, insightful — a challenging programme to implement fasting on an individual and corporate level.

Harold Vaughan
Evangelist and author, founder of Christlife Ministries, USA.

Contents

Acknowledgements	17
Foreword	19
Introduction	23
Part 1 – Before you start	**26**
How to…	26
Stories of transformation	29
Part 2 – How to become ready	**39**
Preparing oneself	39
The end result	48
Part 3 – Start the journey	**52**
Day One – Fasting and prayer according to Jesus	52
Day Two – The right time to fast and pray	60
Day Three – When trouble comes your way	67
Day Four – When God reveals His plan	75
Day Five – God's challenge for spiritual revival	83

Day Six – Waiting for a promise to be fulfilled	90
Day Seven – Decision time in ministry	98
Part 4 – Moving on	**106**
What's next?	106
Appendix 1 – A life of prayer and power	109
Appendix 2 – John Wesley on fasting and prayer	113

Acknowledgements

I am always grateful to God for His mercy and grace. There are no words to express how gracious He has been to me. Since I was a child, I knew the Lord had a purpose for me. I never knew it included moving to Northern Ireland, aged 25, and becoming the pastor of Transformation Centre.

However, since 2006, I can testify to His goodness and blessing. I have seen the church grow, spiritually and numerically. I have been blessed to see many lives transformed by the power of God. He has been gracious to give me a vision for the future of His Church in Ireland. Our purpose is *"to introduce everyone, everywhere, to the transforming power of God – the Gospel."* I continue to look to God for the fulfilment of all His promises regarding the Church.

I am grateful to God for my amazing wife and our three children. Without their support and prayers, I could not do all that I do.

I also thank God for Derek Bird, who, since 2013, has been a constant help as a personal assistant and a great friend. English is my second language, therefore his help in checking and revising this book has been invaluable. I also thank God for Jim Johnston, who has been my spiritual mentor since 2016 and has often challenged me to be everything God wants me to be. He was the one that challenged me to write, and here I am.

Adela Dubei, our church secretary, and Nathan Ivonici, our pastoral assistant, have both been wonderful in giving me the time and space to write. Dr John Haley has been such a blessing by bringing constructive input into this project.

I have been so blessed to have a leadership team of elders and deacons who have placed prayer as the first priority in the church. Their constant example and encouragement have helped shape me as a pastor and leader. Norman Moore's prayer life has been a wonderful inspiration. Aaron Muguti's commitment to fasting has spurred me on to write this book for the good of all God's people.

Finally, I am so thankful to the church community. Since 2006, Transformation Centre has been the source of my greatest joy. I am blessed to be encouraged by the church growth and development, alongside mistakes and successes. Both have been very much part of my spiritual journey, and I look forward to more of what God has for me.

Soli Deo Gloria!
(Glory of God Alone)

Foreword

As I'm writing this foreword, my favourite Major League Baseball team, the Atlanta Braves, are competing in the World Series. I think of a young man who has never played the game, sitting in the stands, watching these finely tuned athletes perform at a world-class level, and hearing the crowd cheering them on like gods. Now imagine him thinking, "You know what? That's a pretty cool gig. I wouldn't mind getting in on that. I think I'll show up tomorrow at the coach's office and let him know I'm ready to join the team." That young man would be in for a rude awakening, to say the least.

It is absurd to think that someone who has never played the game could simply show up and compete at the level of a professional athlete. Any fan of any sport knows it takes years of practice, sweat and dedication to play at that level. And yet, when it comes to the spiritual life, we somehow think, "I've been saved. I've received the Holy Spirit. I'm ready to live like Jesus... *right now.*" That line of thinking is guaranteed to lead to disappointment, disillusionment, or worse.

In his book, *The Spirit of the Disciplines,* Dallas Willard reminds us that if we want to be like Jesus, we have to do the things Jesus did. Jesus regularly left the crowds to find a quiet place to pray. Jesus studied and meditated deeply on the Word of God. And Jesus fasted. If it was important for Jesus to actually do those things, how much more do we need to do them?

If the failure to recognise the vital role spiritual disciplines play in the Christian life is the error of some, others go to the opposite extreme. They turn the disciplines into a Christian "to-do list" with the intent of making sure they check off all the boxes every day, as if checking off the boxes will make them holy and empower them for fruitful Christian living! That is pure legalism and just as powerless as neglecting the disciplines.

I credit Richard Foster with helping me discover the true meaning and purpose of the spiritual disciplines (*Celebration of Discipline*). Foster reminds us that only God, working through the power of the Holy Spirit, can produce the character of Jesus in a person's life. The disciplines are nothing more than the means by which we put ourselves in the presence of God so He can do that work. If we recite words in a prayer, or read a chapter a day in the Bible, or even skip a meal once a week just so we can check it off our list, we have completely missed the point. Prayer is a means of entering into the presence of the living God. Reading and studying the Bible is a means of listening to the voice of God. And fasting is a means of pursuing spiritual nourishment and power by setting aside one of our most basic human needs.

I am thrilled to recommend this practical guide to fasting because it flows directly out of the life of one who has discovered its power through his own personal experience. It is no coincidence that Pastor Nick Serb leads a church that goes by the name "Transformation Centre." Nick's passion is to see the power of God transforming lives, families, cities, and even nations for the glory of God. His commitment to fasting personally and to leading a church that regularly fasts together is one of the reasons they are seeing that vision become a reality.

Read this book, but more importantly, live it. You will be amazed at the difference it makes both in and through you for the glory of God.

Bishop Keith Cowart
Oversee of Free Methodist ministries along the Eastern Seaboard and the South Central United States, as well as in Europe, the Middle East and Asia.

Introduction

There's never been a more opportune time for God's Church to rediscover the power and the blessing of fasting and prayer. As I look around our society, I see the need for a new and fresh move of the Holy Spirit upon His Church.

I grew up in a small town in the central region of Romania. By the time I was born, my father had already been leading a thriving church. Romania was still a communist country, and yet churches were growing at a rapid rate. I treasure the memories of my first experiences in the church prayer meetings. Every Thursday, believers met despite all the risks, praying together for several hours.

We all knelt when praying, something I still do to this day. The wooden floor felt cold and hard to my knees, and although I sat with my father at the front of the church, I would often keep my eyes open to observe everyone praying.

People were emotional in those days, totally unashamed to cry their hearts out before God. They prayed for what seemed like forever. Now as I pastor, I miss those early childhood days of fervent and honest prayer.

Prayer was also part of our home life. I do not remember this particular incident, but my father recalls how he was once deep in prayer in our living room. In the middle of his praying and crying, he felt this little nudge on his shoulder. It was me asking permission to join him. And I did. I knelt down and prayed with him. I was four years old. I grew up with prayer.

Back home, in Romania, our Sunday morning service always started with one hour of prayer. Oh, how I miss the old saints of my childhood and their "lengthy, boring and honest prayers!"

This is one of the reasons I am writing a book on fasting and prayer. Later on, as a teenager, I often heard my father talking about fasting and prayer. To me, fasting seemed a further step into experiencing God. I thought prayer was hard enough – to be frank, fasting sounded impossible.

Maybe you feel the same. Prayer does not often come naturally, and if that is you, the whole idea of fasting may seem even more challenging. But do not worry! You are in good company. Let me just tell you that fasting and prayer can become the most amazing spiritual experience that you could ever have in your personal relationship with God.

All I would ask of you is to take the first step and start the journey with me. Be like a child, curious and willing to try. Most believers and churches indeed struggle when it comes to prayer, never mind fasting. However, we should never resign to such thinking.

Let me offer the following admission. I am entirely aware of the pitfalls of writing anything on fasting and prayer. Any human rule of "don't touch" or "don't eat" can come in direct contradiction to God's Word that says to enjoy food, to eat and drink to the glory of God. Our fasting and prayer are meant to be an act of worship. The end result of your time with God is meant to bring spiritual maturity and joy, not burdens or legalism.

Introduction

This book is meant to be practical. The call to fast and pray is different from your day-to-day prayer time. Every Christian is called to pray daily and develop their relationship with God. Your quiet time / devotional time is necessary as part of your discipleship.

However, there are times when you must go further. That's when you are called to fast and pray. Your decision to fast means that you refrain from food and only drink liquid such as water, tea or coffee. Your fasting is accompanied by prayers of supplication and intercession.

You are encouraged to commit around 40 minutes every day. This includes reading a passage from the Bible and a short devotional. Then spend the remainder of that time in prayer. You can take notes if you wish.

Enough books have been written on prayer to last a lifetime. This book is meant to be a guide to help you create a discipline of fasting and prayer. It is intended to bring glory to God and benefit the Church! It can be used by those who are familiar with fasting and prayer and those who have never fasted and prayed before.

All you need to do is set out your reason for fasting and prayer, decide the time, and do it. If you can get others to join you in your journey, it would be even better. If you have never fasted before, you may want to fast alternate days or choose a day in the week for fasting and prayer.

Part 1

Before you start

How to…

In this book, I invite you and your church to break the status quo and draw closer to God through fasting and prayer. God's promise is that He will draw close to us. Use this book as a guide, not a manual nor an end to all things. This is not a theological essay on fasting and prayer. It is simply a devotional guide to encourage you to do what may seem impossible, fast and pray.

PART 1 – Sets out the plan for the seven days of fasting and prayer. It also includes two stories of transformation. This is an example of how fasting and prayer changed lives and transformed a church.

PART 2 – Invites you to get ready. In this section, you will find some basic ideas on fasting. You will read about what fasting is, its purpose or reason, and what to do during fasting. Then you will explore brokenness, its Biblical understanding, and how you may experience a level of brokenness during your fasting and prayer with the end result being joy.

PART 3 – Contains the devotional material for your seven days of fasting and prayer.

Day One – Will deal with fasting and prayer according to Jesus. We will be looking at Jesus' position on fasting and prayer and why this is different from just prayer.

Day Two – Will consider the subject of the best time for fasting and prayer. Jesus gives us important clues when we need to fast and pray.

Day Three – Will look at fasting and prayer in times of trouble. We know difficult times will come, so we must be ready to face them with fasting and prayer.

Day Four – Will be about fasting and prayer in times of revelation. When God reveals His plan to Daniel, he fasts and prays to see it fulfilled.

Day Five – Will be about the role of fasting and prayer in a spiritual revival. God often calls His people to a spiritual revival through fasting and prayer.

Day Six – Will cover fasting and prayer as we are waiting for a promise of God to be fulfilled. Anna and Simeon will help us understand waiting.

Day Seven – Will teach us about fasting and prayer in times of ministry. Paul, the Apostle, will help us learn how to make important decisions through fasting and prayer.

PART 4 – Looks at what to do after finishing the journey of the Seven Days. You will find a call to evangelism in "the marketplace," an encouragement to a continuous life of prayer and power, as well as an example of what John Wesley used as principles for regular days of fasting and prayer.

Each day you will be encouraged to read the Word of God. You will also be encouraged to think about prayer on your own and with the church. There will be some practical advice on private and public prayer. It is always useful to write things down, especially when you are listening to the voice of the Holy Spirit while you pray.

Stories of Transformation...

Story One

The story began in November 2006. I had just left Romania to come and spend some time with Mount Zion Church in Lisburn, Northern Ireland.

The plan was to spend the night with my dear friends, Stephen and Lisa, in Bangor, then drive the next day to meet the church's leaders and be introduced to the church setting in Lisburn.

I was meant to spend a few weeks with the church, preaching, teaching and doing some pastoral work to test and see what plans God had for me. You may call this period a trial or just a time to explore God's will and direction for the future.

I never had an issue leaving Romania behind. My previous job as an English-teacher in the military school was fulfilling, but I always knew that was not God's plan for my life. There was more. I was nearly convinced that I would stay to serve God in Northern Ireland; however, I needed to be sure. This was the reason for getting on the plane and travelling to Lisburn.

Of all the places, you may ask, why Northern Ireland? At the end of high school I was preparing to go and study in America at a prestigious Christian University when pastor Norman Fox from Lisburn suggested, on one of his visits to our church in Romania, to come and study in Northern Ireland. God put all things together, and I ended up at Belfast

Bible College. Upon graduation, I returned to Romania, and five years later, I found myself back in Lisburn. This time it was different.

On my first day, I was given a tour of the church building. Norman Wright and Ronnie Nesbitt did a good job explaining things, including the church's recent history. It was good to get some information, as the plan was to spend some time serving the church.

I remember clearly, being taken to a side room. They called it "The Prayer Room". At that time, I had no clue that this particular room would be so closely connected with the most wonderful encounters with Jesus I have ever had in my life.

As I walked into the room, I was introduced to Victor Irwin, who was working away, plastering the wall. I encountered a polite, smiling and joyful man. We connected instantly. As we continued the tour I enquired about Victor's situation. I was told he had attended church for a while, but at that moment was away from God. The church was still praying for him. Although he was no longer attending services, he still loved the church and was happy to do work around the building when it was necessary.

I was then taken to the pastor's office. The church hadn't had a pastor for quite a while, so the office was now used as storage space. The dust was everywhere, so I decided to stay behind and tidy the office when the tour finished.

The pastor's office was next door to the Prayer Room, so I went in and offered Victor a cup of coffee. He agreed, and we found ourselves having a good conversation and some laughs. The locals in Northern Ireland would say, "That was good *craic,*" meaning, one was having a good time. I was learning very quickly. I didn't realise that that cup of coffee would be the start of an amazing friendship and would change both of our lives.

It wasn't long into our conversation that I began to feel this was turning into a divine appointment. Coming from a very traditional church background meant it took me a while to discern. However, I could hear this inner voice saying: "Nick, the man you see in front of you will be the first person you will baptise in this place."

I could only assume this was the voice of the Holy Spirit, so I told Victor what my heart was saying. "This may sound strange to you," I said, "But I think you will be the first person I will baptise in this church."

He laughed quite loudly and said: "You must have some faith, pastor. I can't see that happening right now." I told him I would be praying for him; then we returned to our jobs. That day, the Lord put him on my heart in a way I had never experienced before. I gave myself to prayer for Victor and the whole church. The congregation was small, but the Lord was calling me to pray like never before. I remember being awakened during the night to pray for, you know who. This continued for a while until I had to go to see him and say: "Victor, you must get saved so I can get some decent sleep."

During my first weeks there, I fasted and prayed, mostly to know if it were God's will for me to stay and for God to give me a vision for the church. Every Tuesday night, I met with a small group of faithful prayer warriors, seeking God's face with passion and tears. We all knew it was the only way to see the church move forward.

After a while, I was introduced to Irene, Victor's wife. She and her friends had been meeting weekly for many years to fast and pray for her husband. Knowing God's promise, I made Victor's salvation a priority in our prayer times with the church.

I believed God would keep His word about Victor, but there were two problems: Victor was not a Christian, and the church had no baptismal tank. Despite these two issues, I continued to fast and pray for him every Thursday. Others joined me in fasting and prayer.

Norman Moore was eager to introduce the church to long prayer sessions that would last until the early hours of the morning. We did that with joy, and God gave us some amazing blessings in prayer. We pleaded with God for the church, for Victor and the community.

In February 2007, I was finally inducted as the pastor of Mount Zion Free Methodist Church, which later came to be known as Transformation Centre. This came after the Lord had confirmed to me and to the church that this was His will for us. For the following two years, I preached the Gospel with joy. I also continued to pray for Victor, holding on to God's promise.

Norman challenged me during one prayer meeting, asking, "What must God do to save Victor? Let's ask God to do whatever He must do, so Victor could be saved." I agreed. So that night, we poured out our souls to God and asked Him to do whatever He must do.

The following Sunday, Victor was in his garage, on a ladder, getting some tools ready for the next day when he fell and broke his hip. That week I visited him in hospital, and for the first time, we were able to have a heart-to-heart conversation about his soul. Victor took the chance and opened his heart to me. It was the first time he had ever done that. I shared the Gospel and encouraged him to confess his sins to God, ask His forgiveness, and come to Him. At the end of my visit, I prayed and left my Bible with him. "You need it more than I do," I said and left the hospital praying.

It wasn't long after that Victor got home on crutches. I clearly remember one Sunday morning around 10.30 am when I had a phone call from Irene. "Come quickly," she said, "Victor is not well; he did not sleep at all last night." I had one shoe on already. I put the other shoe on, jumped in the car and drove to their house just outside Lisburn.

I found Victor in the conservatory, sitting in an armchair. His two crutches were by his side, and he was crying uncontrollably. I stopped in the doorway, and as I looked at him, I began to weep with joy. I knew God had been there before me.

"Pastor Nick," he muttered, "it's time God takes over Victor Irwin's life!" Tears filled our eyes as we read the Bible together, prayed together and cried with joy. That morning Victor entered the Kingdom of God and was transformed forever.

Following his conversion, he burned his bridges with sin, and God began healing the family from the hurt and consequences of a sinful past. It was shortly after that the church got a baptism tank. It was Victor who not only built it, but he and Irene paid for it. When it was completed, both of them were the first to be baptised in front of a packed church. There was not one dry eye that night.

Visitor's transformation caused a domino effect in his family and the church. God was gracious, and one by one, family members came to the Lord. Many believed, because they witnessed what God had done in Victor as an answer to prayer. God used him to bring many to Christ as he began to share the Gospel with those around him. Today, he leads prayer meetings in the church, in the very Prayer Room where people used to pray for his salvation.

We still fast and pray for others. We do not give up. There are so many more, just like Victor who need to know Jesus. This story is just one example of how God used fasting and prayer to prove to us that He is listening.

Story Two

Have you ever wondered if your prayers will ever be answered? As much as we want our prayers answered right away, sometimes God seems to take His time in giving us the answer we want.

During my time in Lisburn, I had the great privilege of meeting great people of prayer. One of them was John Mackin. Unfortunately, I did not have much time with him before his passing, but his impact on the church was significant. He was one of the church's founding members, and he considered prayer to be one of his life's callings.

John prayed for his nephew Robert for 65 years. During all this time, very little seemed to have happened. By the time I came to the church, he had been an alcoholic for 50 years. His first drink was at age ten on a Sunday school trip, when some older boys thought it would be funny to get him drunk. Over time he became addicted to alcohol to such a degree that he could not live without it. He was once thrown out of Lagan Valley Hospital for smuggling in alcohol. On another occasion, he showed up at an Alcoholics Anonymous meeting but because he arrived drunk they politely asked him not to attend until he was sober. His driving licence was suspended for driving under the influence, being ten times over the limit. He escaped jail on a technicality.

Despite all this, Robert kept attending his family church faithfully, every Sunday. However, he never related to anything that was being said. To him, church was just a "tick a box" exercise, and that's it. Once home, he would go back to drinking his eight bottles of Vodka per week.

His alcoholism came with a great price. He had no self-esteem left, and life was just a monotonous routine of drinking, feeling sorry for himself and more drinking until, one day, God spoke to him in a most peculiar way.

Previously, Robert had found a little plaque that someone had thrown away. It had the words of the Apostle Paul: "My grace is sufficient for thee." He brought it home and hung it above his fireplace, and it stayed there for years until this particular day.

The day had started like every other, with much drinking to the point of misery and depression. He sat in his living room armchair with a bottle of Vodka beside him. A voice in his head was saying: "Do it! End it all right now!" In time the whisper turned into taunting: "You cannot do it! You are such a coward!" He fought the voice for a couple of hours, running up and down the stairs. He was desperate and broken. He cried until his chest was sore. Then God spoke to him.

Robert looked at the plaque on his wall and found great comfort. He heard God say: "Come to Me, and come now! Tomorrow might be too late!" He replied: "Yes, I am coming. But what do I do now" The Lord replied: "Get up and go to the church next door." And he did. He came in just as he was; broken and desperate.

I remember that day so clearly; he came in and sat on the last row of pews, which was always empty. I preached like I always did, with passion and commitment. Later on, he told me that every word I said applied to him as if I knew everything about his life. However, this was only part of the miracle.

At the end of the service, we sang our last hymn. As he joined in he felt something like electricity going through his whole body, from his head to his toes. There was no one beside him; no one laid hands on him and no one prayed over him. It was God and God alone. At the end of the service Robert approached Victor (the man from the first story) and told him what happened. Victor smiled and said: "It is the Holy Spirit! God touched you!"

That day, all of "Uncle John's" prayers were answered. "Uncle John" received the news while in the hospital. The doctors had told the family that he would be gone by the end of that week. The good news seemed have to given him a new lease of life as he lived on for three more years and died peacefully at the wonderful age of 95. Robert came into our church completely broken and desperate. He left completely healed and saved. As he went out he stopped the first person he met, and said, "I just got saved"! No one believed him. Two weeks later, he was still talking about it. So people began to take him seriously.

That same week he joined us in the prayer meeting. I gave him a Bible and asked him to pray. He told me in no uncertain terms: "If you ask me again to read and pray, I will never come back to this church again." I told him that God is working in him and to trust me that everything would be ok.

Believe it or not, Robert reads the Bible with vigour every day. And not only that, he prays and leads an early prayer meeting in my office every Friday morning with a wonderful prayer team. He also leads prayer meetings for the Christian Workers Union in Lisburn.

Not long after his transformation, Robert came to see me. He had a letter from his doctor asking him to present himself to his surgery for further tests. The doctor had heard what had happened, and was worried for Robert's health. It was anticipated that he would suffer severe withdrawal symptoms following his long alcoholism. Robert asked me: "What do I do with this Pastor Nick? I have no withdrawal symptoms! God healed me!"

I told Robert to go and see the doctor and tell him everything that had happened. And so he did. His testimony has had such an impact that people today still stop me in the middle of the town to ask me about Robert, more than ten years after his conversion.

Robert's transformed life led his neighbour, Sandra, to come to know Jesus. The Lord also miraculously transformed her life, freed her from the bondage of alcohol, and she is now a church representative with Release International for the persecuted Church. We will keep her story for another day.

Robert's family is attending church, and he prays for them, just like "Uncle John" prayed for him. One day God will answer his prayers, and in the meantime, He is empowering Robert for more and more. Never stop praying.

Part 2
How to become ready
Preparing Oneself

The purpose of this book is to equip you and your church to go deeper with God in fasting and prayer. Be aware that any activity can become a ritual and therefore void of spiritual significance. We are to resist mechanical and ritualistic worship.

For Jesus, fasting and prayer was the way to prepare Himself for ministry. It was the Holy Spirit that led Him in the wilderness to be tested. After 40 days and nights of fasting and prayer, he returned, victorious and filled with the power of the Holy Spirit.

Paul, the Apostle, is also a similar example. After encountering the resurrected Jesus, he spent three days in Damascus, fasting and praying, waiting for Ananias to come and baptise him. His desire for God had become so intense, that for the three days he could only fast and pray.

Begin by asking a simple question. What do I want God to do for me? This may sound like a silly question, but take a moment to think about it. In life, we prioritise what we assume to be important. We seldom miss appointments we consider vital to our life. So, begin this journey by searching your heart.

If you read Isaiah 58, you'll see that God is rebuking the people of Israel because of their lack of honesty in their worship. Prayer had become ritualistic and void of reality. Fasting was, for most of them, a pious act without any meaning. And they were wondering why God was not answering their prayers. Isaiah dedicates a whole chapter to correct the thinking of God's people regarding fasting and prayer. This is where we must begin.

What is fasting?

I understand spiritual fasting as abstinence from food with the purpose of devoting the time to feed your soul with God's Word. Some people also fast by abstaining from social media, TV and other basic necessities or luxuries. In his letter to the church in Corinth, the Apostle Paul suggests that during times of prayer, couples should refrain from sexual intimacy as a way of focusing on the spiritual needs rather than the physical.

"Do not deprive each other of sexual relations, unless you both agree to refrain from sexual intimacy for a limited time so you can give yourselves more completely to prayer. Afterward, you should come together again so that Satan won't be able to tempt

you because of your lack of self-control" 1 Corinthians 7:5. We know that social media is one of the greatest distractions in our lives, and refraining from it can be a real test of commitment and dedication to the things of God.

Drawing closer to God in prayer and abstaining from food while you pray will teach you self-control. This is a special time of supplication and intercession when you can plead with God with a specific purpose in mind.

Fasting and prayer are spiritual disciplines. However, according to *healthline.com* there are some amazing physical benefits for both. Fasting is a practice associated with a wide array of potential health benefits, including weight loss, as well as improved blood sugar control, heart health, brain function and cancer prevention. *"When fasting, be sure to stay hydrated, eat nutrient-dense foods and get plenty of rest. It's best to consult with your doctor before fasting if you have any underlying health conditions or are planning to fast for more than 24 hours."* [1]

It is vital to mention that if you suffer from a medical condition which demands that you eat at regular times, it is wise to consult your doctor before you embark on this journey of fasting.

Some people with medical conditions, who still want to take this journey, have found it useful to start fasting right after their evening meal and not eat until the next morning. For example, if you finish eating at 5.00 pm you can set time aside to pray, read the Bible and worship God before you

---

1 https://www.healthline.com/nutrition/fasting-benefits#section11

go to bed. You will be fasting for 16 hours if your breakfast is at 9.00 am. You can have another time of prayer, reading and worshipping God as you start the new day. Be wise and take medical advice if you need it.

What is the purpose of fasting and prayer?

The primary purpose of fasting and prayer is the development of your spiritual life and closeness to God. Fasting and prayer are acts of worship. However, during times of fasting and prayer, you may determine in your heart to overcome a particular habitual sin. You may have other reasons too. For example, you may fast and pray for the salvation of a loved one, the healing of a person who is sick, or a breakthrough in your daily walk with God.

Fasting and prayer with the church develops unity and fosters love more than any other activity. God commands His blessing upon those who live in unity. He also answers the prayers of those who come to Him in agreement. If you want unity in the church, get people to fast and pray together.

In Mark 9, we find the story of a father who brings his son to the disciples to be healed. The story tells us how an evil spirit throws the boy into the water and fire, trying to kill him. The disciples are puzzled when they try to cast out the demon, but they fail.

Later on, Jesus explains why they couldn't heal the boy. It wasn't because they had no authority or power. It was simply because "this kind" doesn't come out, except with fasting and prayer. This story teaches us that there are victories that are pretty easy to win. However, there are times when we are called to go much deeper in order to find victory. Fasting and prayer take you deeper and further with God.

From Mark 9, we conclude that fasting and prayer act as spiritual weapons. These powerful weapons must be an integral part of the spiritual arsenal in every believer who seriously considers living a life of victory.

Paul mentions such "mighty weapons" in his second letter to the church in Corinth: *"We are human, but we don't wage war as humans do. Instead, we use God's mighty weapons, not worldly weapons, to knock down the strongholds of human reasoning and to destroy false arguments. We destroy every proud obstacle that keeps people from knowing God. We capture their rebellious thoughts and teach them to obey Christ"* 2 Corinthians 10:3–5.

As believers, we do not fight against flesh-and-blood enemies. The warfare we are involved in is spiritual therefore we must be equipped accordingly: *"A final word: Be strong in the Lord and in his mighty power. Put on all of God's armour so that you will be able to stand firm against all strategies of the devil. For we are not fighting against flesh-and-blood enemies, but against evil rulers and authorities of the unseen world, against mighty powers in this dark world, and against evil spirits in the heavenly places"* Ephesians 6:10–12.

Unless adequately equipped, we are prone to lose the fight every time the devil opposes us. Fasting and prayer prepares and trains us how to use our spiritual armour. *"Therefore, put on every piece of God's armour so you will be able to resist the enemy in the time of evil. Then after the battle you will still be standing firm. Stand your ground, putting on the belt of truth and the body armour of God's righteousness. For shoes, put on the peace that comes from the Good News so that you will be fully prepared. In addition to all of these, hold up the shield of faith to stop the fiery arrows of the devil. Put on salvation as your helmet, and take the sword of the Spirit, which is the word of God"* Ephesians 6:13–17.

The context of putting on the armour of God is the topic of prayer. That is why the Apostle Paul finishes this section with a call to prayer. *"Pray in the Spirit at all times and on every occasion. Stay alert and be persistent in your prayers for all believers everywhere"* Ephesians 6:18.

Fasting and prayer should have a spiritual reason. You can have ***a personal reason,*** such as overcoming a struggle, sin, or dealing with family sickness. Or you may have a need to develop discipline and self-control as a fruit of the Holy Spirit. As a church, you can have ***a corporate reason*** for your fasting and prayer. For example, you may fast and pray for your community, church ministries or the church leadership.

In Transformation Centre, we try to dedicate at least one week to fast and pray for the year ahead. We have experienced great blessing every time we prioritised fasting and prayer above any other ministry or activity. It is a good practice to unify the church around a common purpose.

What should I do during fasting?

Pray. Set aside time and plan your prayer time. Take notes as you plan. It is useful to develop a good and healthy habit of keeping a prayer diary. This is true for you as an individual but also as a church. You can look back and see the prayers that have been answered. Pray and listen to the Holy Spirit.

Read. Set aside time to read the Word of God. A significant purpose of fasting is that you recognise the value of God's Word. *"People do not live by bread alone, but by every word that comes from the mouth of God"* Matthew 4:4b. Let the Word feed your soul just like physical food feeds your body. During this time, you may study a portion of Scripture concerning your reason for fasting. If you fast and pray to overcome an addiction, read passages where God speaks about it. For example:

"You say, 'I am allowed to do anything'—but not everything is good for you. And even though 'I am allowed to do anything,' I must not become a slave to anything" 1 Corinthians 6:12.

"So then, since we have a great High Priest who has entered heaven, Jesus the Son of God, let us hold firmly to what we believe. This High Priest of ours understands our weaknesses, for he faced all of the same testings we do, yet he did not sin. So let us come boldly to the throne of our gracious God. There we will receive his mercy, and we will find grace to help us when we need it most" Hebrews 4:14–16.

Praise. Choose to praise and worship God while you fast and pray. Worship is an act of prayerful meditation. You can easily do this in song. The act of worship is often linked to the attitude of brokenness when one prostrates oneself before God. Every church should develop a culture where this is possible. Praising is helping you build contentment in your heart. Praise is the decision to honour God, no matter what the circumstances. Hungry or full, thirsty or satisfied, in every situation, learn to praise God.

Fellowship. Fasting and prayer can sometimes be hard, especially when the devil comes to oppose you. If, as a church, you decide to take time to fast and pray together, take the opportunity to be with other believers for prayer, fellowship and mutual encouragement. Do not neglect fellowship with other believers whether you fast and pray on your own or with the church. It will be a great source of encouragement.

Chapter Summary

Let me conclude this part by saying categorically that fasting and prayer does not save a person. Fasting and prayer is for those who have already experienced God's salvation. Fasting and prayer is your worship to God, an act of the will already submitted to the lordship of Jesus.

Some people may think that fasting for long periods and praying long prayers will be a way to force God into doing something for you. No! Fasting and prayer simply shows your determination to get close to God, with obedience and submission to His sovereign will. Penance or self-pity will not buy you grace. Salvation, the Word of God says, is by faith alone. Jesus calls us to repent and turn away from sin. We are called to confess with our mouth the lordship of Jesus and believe in our hearts that God raised Him from the dead. This wonderful work of grace in our lives is salvation.

Be blessed as you determine in your heart to draw close to God in fasting and prayer! My prayer is that as the Church returns to the practice of fasting and prayer, God will hear us and revive us.

Revival is the work of the Holy Spirit, turning the lukewarm church and lukewarm Christians into spiritually "highly flammable" followers of Jesus. The Holy Spirit can turn an indifferent Christian into a compassionate and loving person.

We understand that the Holy Spirit is here for this age of grace. We stand forgiven, and there is no more condemnation for those who are in Christ Jesus. Revival starts in the heart. It changes the spiritual atmosphere in the church, and then, ultimately, it affects the community around us. Revival begins here and it must begin on a personal level.

That is why we choose to fast and pray!

The End Result

Brokenness is often looked upon as something negative. Broken things are easily disposed of, rejected and deemed useless. However, God uses brokenness and weakness in order to display His power and majesty.

As you study the Bible, you will find that fasting and prayer is often associated with brokenness of heart or spirit. David tells us in Psalm 51:16–17 that God desires a broken spirit and a contrite heart, much more than sacrifices: *"You do not desire a sacrifice, or I would offer one. You do not want a burnt offering. The sacrifice you desire is a broken spirit. You will not reject a broken and repentant heart, O God."*

Brokenness must not be misunderstood as self-punishment or being hard on yourself in an attempt to appease God. Biblical brokenness is an attitude of the heart, a decision we make as a response to God's work in our hearts. It is often reflected by humility or being "humble before God." In Daniel 10, we read about the prophet being broken over the future events the Lord had shown him in the previous chapter. He was fasting and praying, humbling himself before God when God revealed Himself and reassured Daniel: *"… you are very precious to God, so listen carefully to what I have to say to you. Stand up, for I have been sent to you"* Daniel 10:11.

I see at least three types of brokenness in the Bible:

Brokenness over unconfessed sin

When the Holy Spirit convicts us of sin, we must be broken over it. We cannot allow our hearts to become calloused and accustomed to sinning. The conviction of the Holy Spirit brings brokenness. Holy brokenness brings repentance. Repentance brings forgiveness, and forgiveness brings joy. Can you see it? The end result of brokenness is joy! Once a sin is confessed and forgiven, we can no longer be broken over it. We must rejoice in our forgiveness. For example, the church in Corinth had to experience this brokenness to experience repentance and then forgiveness.

"I am not sorry that I sent that severe letter to you, though I was sorry at first, for I know it was painful to you for a little while. Now I am glad I sent it, not because it hurt you, but because the pain caused you to repent and change your ways. It was the kind of sorrow God wants his people to have, so you were not harmed by us in any way. For the kind of sorrow God wants us to experience leads us away from sin and results in salvation. There's no regret for that kind of sorrow. But worldly sorrow, which lacks repentance, results in spiritual death" 2 Corinthians 7:8–10.

Brokenness in intercession

This is a different kind of brokenness. Numerous intercessors in the Bible felt broken over the spiritual state of other people or their nation. Nehemiah was broken over the state of Jerusalem and its walls. Daniel was broken over the events predicted by God. Jesus wept over Jerusalem. You can be broken over your friend's sin or sickness. That state of brokenness and intercession will bring you to fasting and prayer. As you do, the Lord gives you peace and the result of the intercession is joy. The end result of intercession is joy!

Brokenness in need

The Lord Jesus told us in John 16:33 to expect trials and sorrows in this world: *"Here on earth you will have many trials and sorrows. But take heart, because I have overcome the world."* We know that our needy world is heading towards judgment. This truth should be enough to break our hearts. This brokenness is crucial for compassion. Compassion cannot exist without brokenness. The Bible tells us that Jesus had compassion for people, and therefore ministered to their needs.

"Jesus saw the huge crowd as he stepped from the boat, and he had compassion on them and healed their sick" Matthew 14:14.

"Jesus saw the huge crowd as he stepped from the boat, and he had compassion on them because they were like sheep without a shepherd. So he began teaching them many things" Mark 6:34.

Jesus wept with people. He wept at the tomb of His friend Lazarus. He identified with the brokenness of those around Him and sympathised with their pain. In Gethsemane, just before His arrest, Jesus prayed for His disciples and wept while His sweat became like drops of blood. He knew that after His departure, the disciples would face innumerable obstacles and trials, so He prayed with their needs in mind.

Chapter Summary

What do we do when we are faced with our own sin, the spiritual state of our nation or a personal and immediate need? We bring it all to God with fasting and prayer. Whatever we face, whether it be salvation, healing, provision, or a new revelation from His Word; once we bring it to God, we leave it with God. This will teach us how to depend on Him. When we leave the matter with God, the end result is joy.

The end result of brokenness is always joy. God's purpose for us is to have full and complete joy. Fasting and prayer is all about joy. We can rejoice in suffering, we can rejoice in tears, we can rejoice in intercession and in brokenness!

Let the Lord make you willing to be broken during the time of fasting and prayer. If He breaks your heart, He will heal it. His purpose for you is to find joy throughout this journey. *Are you ready?*

Part 3
Start the journey

Day One
Fasting and Prayer according to Jesus

Today's reading: Matthew 6:1-18.

In the Sermon on the Mount, Jesus addresses several topics related to living a godly life. Fasting and prayer is one of those topics. His take on the subject must have shocked the crowds and annoyed the religious elite.

If you read the Gospels carefully, you will notice that Jesus often came into conflict with the religious establishment of His time. The point of conflict was the man-made tradition (the Talmud) that had been added to the commands of God and treated as divine in origin. These human traditions had been embraced while the commands of God had been discarded.

Jesus, as a teacher, was different. He spoke with power and authority and could relate to people's needs. Moreover, his preaching was accompanied by miraculous deeds.

Jesus also had love and compassion for the crowds. The religious leaders of the time were cold and distant. Their teaching was often irrelevant and filled with burdensome requirements.

The Good News of Jesus was a simple but powerful message. He called on people to repent and turn away from their sins. He also announced the imminent arrival of God's Kingdom. His teaching was practical and answered real questions. Unlike the teaching of the Pharisees, the words of Jesus brought freedom.

Jesus used the Pharisees, the religious elite of the time, as an example of what spirituality should not be like. In the area of prayer especially, this is true. In Matthew 6, Jesus talks about prayer and fasting by attacking the hypocrisy of the Pharisees. He is loud and clear: "do not pray or fast like them."

Jesus begins by focusing more on the importance of private prayer. The Pharisees were addicted to pious displays of religiosity by seeking public places to pray so everyone could see them. Jesus is not belittling the importance of public prayer. He simply states that public prayer must come out of your private prayer.

His emphasis is on the prayer room, the hidden and private time with God, which will be rewarded publicly. Jesus challenges us to be on our own with the Father.

"When you pray, don't be like the hypocrites who love to pray publicly on street corners and in the synagogues where everyone

can see them. I tell you the truth, that is all the reward they will ever get. But when you pray, go away by yourself, shut the door behind you, and pray to your Father in private. Then your Father, who sees everything, will reward you" Matthew 6:5–6.

There is no point in displaying great piety and spirituality in the public arena if our private prayer is non-existent. In fact, our public prayer should reflect our private prayer.

In private, we can pour out our hearts to God in a way that is nearly impossible in public. But if we grow in our relationship with God by private prayer, we will be ready and willing to unite with others in public prayer.

Pray like this …

Jesus goes on to give us a "model prayer." It is not a prayer that we should repeat over and over again. That would go against His specific instruction: *"When you pray, don't babble on and on as the Gentiles do. They think their prayers are answered merely by repeating their words again and again. Don't be like them, for your Father knows exactly what you need even before you ask him!"* Matthew 6:7–8.

The "model prayer" gives us a structure on which to build. It is more of a pattern than a substitute for our own words. Warren Wiersbe gives a wonderful explanation on how this prayer could be used: *"The purpose of prayer is to glorify God's name, to ask for help to accomplish His will on earth. This prayer begins with God's interest, not ours: God's name, God's Kingdom and God's will. We should not ask God for anything that will dishonour His name, delay His Kingdom, or disturb*

His will on earth. Note that this prayer contains no singular pronouns; they are all plural. It begins with 'Our Father.' When we pray, we must remember we are part of God's worldwide family of believers." [2]

Once we put God's interests first, seeking His glory, His Kingdom and His honour; we can then bring our own needs to Him. These personal needs cover our daily bread, the forgiveness of our sins, the potential to be tempted and fall, and ultimately, our desire to be rescued from the evil one.

At the end of this section, Jesus links prayer with forgiveness. There are times when we all pray for the forgiveness of our sins. Jesus makes it clear that our forgiveness is closely linked to our forgiveness of others. We forgive others because we have been forgiven. This is grace. We approach God in prayer with the joy of His forgiveness. As we experience His forgiveness and grace, we cannot but forgive others.

Fasting and prayer is meant to shape our character and attitude — especially our attitude towards those who sin against us. When we fast and pray for such situations, with all honesty and openness of heart, we are empowered to forgive.

Our character must catch up with our calling. It is part of the making of every man and woman of God. This calling is a mighty and great privilege. It comes with a tremendous responsibility. God's calling requires a godly character. When we forgive our fellow men and women, our character is shaped, and we are sanctified. When we forgive, we become more like Jesus.

---

[2] Warren Wiersbe, Transformation Study Bible, "Pray like this" page 1612, David Cook, Supplementary material 2009

Fast like this ...

Fasting and prayer were not new practices for Jesus. Historically, Israel had been used to "solemn assemblies" (Judges 21:5; Nehemiah 8:18), when the religious leaders of that time would call the whole nation to fast and pray regularly. The Pharisees were proud of their weekly fasting and their generous giving.

However, Jesus' teaching on fasting and prayer is different because it is not focused on the visible form of the activity itself but the heart motivation behind it. It's not whether we fast and pray. It's more about why we fast and pray and when we decide to do it. We cannot pray, fast, or give for personal glory or to be seen and appreciated by others. We must do all these things to the glory of God.

Chapter Summary

Fasting and prayer, according to Jesus, is a matter of the heart. It is an act of worship to God who can see in secret and will reward publicly. Fasting and prayer, therefore, begins in the private space. Out of that intimacy with God comes great joy.

That is why Jesus doesn't want us to look miserable and dishevelled when we fast. We should be filled with joy and peace. Meeting with God in private is the most important aspect of our fasting. The expressions "when you pray" and "when you fast" clearly reflect the expectation Jesus had for us, His disciples. It is not "if" you fast and pray, but "when" you fast and pray.

Remember that when Jesus taught His disciples to fast and pray, He wasn't creating a new idea. He was building on a timeless practice — a practice the Pharisees had abandoned for the sake of public honour and false religiosity.

Our fasting and prayer must be different. According to Jesus, we must not do it for show or spiritual pedigree. It must be done for the glory of God and with joy.

Day One

Personal Focus

Set some time aside to reflect on the words of Jesus in Matthew 6:1–18. Allow His words to adjust and correct how you see fasting and prayer. Maybe you need to come up with a plan, a place and a time for regular private prayer.

Use the space below to note down your reflections and your plan.

Public Focus

Prepare to fast and pray as a church. Take some time to discuss the place of public prayer in the life of the church. Jesus said His house must be *"a house of prayer for all nations."* It may be that we as a church must recommit to give ourselves to fasting and prayer for the spiritual vitality of the church.

I've always believed that church must be led from the prayer room and not the board room. Take some notes as you pray and discuss the role of prayer in the church.

Day Two
The right time to fast and pray

Today's reading: Mark 2:18–22.

The question, "when should I fast?" is as trivial as the question, "when should I eat?" You eat when you feel the need to eat. So therefore, you fast when you feel the need to fast.

In Mark 2:18, Jesus is approached by the disciples of John the Baptist with a serious allegation. The disciples of Jesus were not seen to be fasting like everyone else.

Please notice their specific expectation to fast, ***just like everyone else***. It seems fasting and prayer was a set habit and a cultural expectation among the religious elite. If you were part of the religious community, you were expected to fast several times a week. In Jesus' time, fasting and prayer had become so ritualistic and burdensome that most Pharisees were fasting out of habit and routine.

We know this from Luke 18, when Jesus tells the story of two men going to pray: one is a Pharisee and the other a tax collector. Notice the importance of fasting in the prayer of the Pharisee: *"I thank you, God, that I am not like other people—cheaters, sinners, adulterers. I'm certainly not like that tax collector!* ***I fast twice a week****, and I give you a tenth of my income"* Luke 18:11–12.

Jesus points to the prayer of the Pharisee and concludes that it brings no justification. It is pointless. On the contrary, Jesus seems to encourage the humble and broken attitude of the tax collector, who does not dare look up. He keeps his distance and prays, beating his chest in sorrow: *"O God, be merciful to me, for I am a sinner."* Despite the Pharisee's attitude to fasting and prayer, it is important to notice that Jesus does not discourage fasting.

At the start of our journey, we looked at brokenness and how important it is to humble ourselves before God and prepare to fast and pray. It's not about how many times a week you fast; it's not about how long you fast. It's not even about whether you fast at all; it's more about what you do when you decide to fast and pray.

In our reading for today, we find Jesus responding to the allegations made against His disciples. Jesus simply states: *"Do wedding guests fast while celebrating with the groom? Of course not. They can't fast while the groom is with them. But someday the groom will be taken away from them, and then they will fast"* Mark 2:19–20.

So, the best time to fast is when you need to go further with God. The Lord clarifies that there will be a time when He will no longer be with His disciples. Our groom, the Lord Jesus Christ, is no longer here on the earth. So we understand that **NOW** is the best time for the church to fast and pray.

Jesus builds his defence by using three illustrations. The first is a wedding. His argument is simple: you cannot expect the friends of the bridegroom to fast while he is still around. In other words, Jesus confirms that there is a time to rejoice and party, and there is a time to fast and be broken.

The disciples were meant to rejoice in the presence of Jesus just like friends rejoice in the presence of a bridegroom preparing for his wedding day. Jesus also confirms that there will be a day when the bridegroom will no longer be there. In fact, Jesus says, "the bridegroom will be taken away." Those will be the days to fast and pray.

"Jesus replied, 'Do wedding guests fast while celebrating with the groom? Of course not. They can't fast while the groom is with them. But someday the groom will be taken away from them, and then they will fast."

The second illustration used by Jesus is the patching of an old garment using new cloth. People were used to patching old clothes, as only the rich and powerful could afford new clothes. It was therefore not unusual to see people wearing patched clothes.

"Besides, who would patch old clothing with new cloth? For the new patch would shrink and rip away from the old cloth, leaving an even bigger tear than before" Mark 2:21.

The lesson here is that the old way of fasting (ritualistic and legalistic) would do more harm than good. There is a new way to please God and a new way to fast and pray.

The same lesson is reinforced in the third illustration Jesus used. *"And no one puts new wine into old wineskins. For the wine would burst the wineskins, and the wine and the skins would both be lost. New wine calls for new wineskins"* Mark 2:22.

The old way of fasting, the way of the Pharisees, was never God's idea. Their way of fasting is like patching an old cloth with new material or putting new wine into old wineskins. In both examples, the end result is disaster and waste.

There was a time when the disciples did not have to worry about anything. Jesus was there to walk with them, teach them, save them from storms and drowning, or feed them when they were hungry.

While Jesus was with His disciples, there was no need for them to fast. However, the time would come for Him to leave and return to the Father. It was in His absence that the disciples were to exercise faith. This faith would only grow and develop as the disciples fasted and prayed. It was true that they would not be left as orphans. In John 16-18, Jesus gives them the promise of the Holy Spirit. He would be their Helper and Advocate. But they would still need to fast and pray.

In Romans 8, the Apostle Paul reinforces the role and ministry of the Holy Spirit. He will not just be with us but He will help us pray when we do not know how to pray. This is an amazing assurance that we are not alone as we pray.

"And the Holy Spirit helps us in our weakness. For example, we don't know what God wants us to pray for. But the Holy Spirit prays for us with groanings that cannot be expressed in words. And the Father who knows all hearts knows what the Spirit is saying, for the Spirit pleads for us believers in harmony with God's own will" Romans 8:26–27.

Another amazing truth in this passage from Romans 8 is that the Holy Spirit pleads for us in harmony with God's will. It is in the context of God's will that the next verse comes to confirm even more that we are not alone in prayer.

"And we know that God causes everything to work together for the good of those who love God and are called according to his purpose for them" Romans 8:28.

Chapter Summary

Fasting and prayer, done Jesus' way, develops faith. We learn to trust God and depend on Him for our basic needs. When we fast, we worship God. When we pray, we worship God. We do not go on a "hunger strike" to force God's hand. We do not fast out of religious duty; we fast out of joy. We fast to give ourselves to God. We do all this because there are far greater joys in God.

When should I fast? Every time you need to! This should cause us to explore our own spiritual needs and reflect on our relationship with God. Do you need victory in your spiritual life? Fast and pray for it. The best time to fast is when you want to go further with God.

Day Two

Personal Focus

Take some time to reflect on the words of Jesus in Mark 2. Do not rush away. Think about your priorities and assess how sincere is your need for God. Do you want to go further with God? Make a list of the things you want to fast and pray about this week.

Use the space below to write down your reasons for fasting and praying.

Public Focus

Take some time to discuss some of the spiritual priorities of the church with one another. It could be the youth or children's ministry. Perhaps, you need to fast and pray for a new pastor (providing your church doesn't have one). If you have one, fast and pray for the one you have.

Following your discussion, in love and honesty, write down the spiritual priorities of the church as you fast and pray. Agree to pray in unity.

Day Three
When trouble comes your way

Today's reading: 2 Chronicles 20.

No one is immune from trouble. We all face dangers from within and without. We are aware of the fact we cannot control most of the circumstances coming our way. But what we can do, is control our reaction to them.

In 2 Chronicles 17, we read about Jehoshaphat becoming king following the death of his father, Asa. In his early years, Asa had followed God. He had led Judah through some incredible spiritual reforms.

When in trouble, Asa sought God, and God gave him amazing strength against his enemies. The Lord rescued Asa from danger when the Ethiopians came up against Judah. However, towards the end of his life, Asa turned from God and trusted the king of Aram instead. Even on his death bed, suffering from a foot disease, Asa did not seek God but only sought the help of his physicians. It is a sad ending to a life that showed so much promise.

In 2 Chronicles 20, we find Jehoshaphat facing an imminent and unexpected danger. The Moabites, the Ammonites and the Meunites have united against Judah. The king is told that their united armies are already on their way. Although Jehoshaphat is a great military man, we are told in verse 3 he "was terrified."

Jehoshaphat responds to this threatening circumstance in a way that honours God and sets Judah on the path to victory. *"Jehoshaphat was terrified by this news and begged the Lord for guidance. He also ordered everyone in Judah to begin fasting. So people from all the towns of Judah came to Jerusalem to seek the Lord's help"* 2 Chronicles 20:3–4.

As far as I can see, the first time fasting is mentioned in the Bible is regarding to great danger, pain and trouble. In Judges 19, the tribe of Benjamin committed a terrible sin. A man from the tribe of Levi and his concubine stopped in Gibeah, one of the towns belonging to the tribe of Benjamin. They stopped for shelter and overnight rest, thinking it was much safer than any other foreign town. However, during the night, there was trouble: *"While they were enjoying themselves, a crowd of troublemakers from the town surrounded the house. They began beating at the door and shouting to the old man, "Bring out the man who is staying with you so we can have sex with him."*

It is unthinkable that such sin is found among the people whom God rescued from Egypt with a mighty hand. Following their lust and immorality, they killed the man's concubine. In an act of rage and depravity, the man from the tribe of Levi cut her body in 12 pieces and sent them to all the tribes of Israel. There was general outrage against Benjamin. We are told that the rest of the tribes tried twice to punish this sin, but they failed both times. Following their failed attempts, the people of God sought His face for an answer by fasting and prayer. *"Then all the Israelites went up to Bethel and wept in the presence of the Lord and fasted until evening. They also brought burnt offerings and peace offerings to the Lord. The Israelites went up seeking direction from the Lord. (In those days the Ark of the Covenant of God was in Bethel)"* Judges 20:26–27.

This was a dark and unforgettable blemish in the history of God's people. When faced with sin and difficulty, God's people fasted and prayed, and God delivered them. It was exactly what Jehoshaphat did when facing trouble and difficulty. This unexpected attack could mean the end of Judah. In desperation, Israel turned to God.

Jehoshaphat called for a time of fasting and prayer

This seems to be Jehoshaphat's first and only reaction. There was no time to waste; Jehoshaphat called for immediate fasting and prayer. The whole nation responded to the call, and men, women and children gathered before God. They fasted and prayed. There was great brokenness among God's people; it was a desperate and needy time. In such times, the whole nation learnt to depend on God again.

Jehoshaphat led the nation in prayer

At this difficult time, the king assumed a very public place. *"Jehoshaphat stood before the community of Judah and Jerusalem in front of the new courtyard at the Temple of the Lord. He prayed..."* 2 Chronicles 20:5.

Jehoshaphat led Judah in prayer, and his prayer was filled with some amazing truths: He began by praising God (v.6). Then the king claimed the promises God made to Solomon at the dedication of the Temple (v.6–8), and in the end, he presented the issue to God, with a sincere and desperate request for help (v.10–12).

His prayer came straight from the heart. Jehoshaphat, like many other men and women of God, took a trip down memory lane and reminded God of His faithfulness in the past. God's mighty acts of redemption were the basis of Jehoshaphat's request. If God had helped in the past, He would do it again because He is God and never changes.

Jehoshaphat led in worship

Jehoshaphat's prayer united the nation. God responded to their prayer and unity through the voice of a prophet. There was good news: *"Listen, all you people of Judah and Jerusalem! Listen, King Jehoshaphat! This is what the Lord says: Do not be afraid! Don't be discouraged by this mighty army, for the battle is not yours, but God's. Tomorrow, march out against them. You will find them coming up through the ascent of Ziz at the end of the valley that opens into the wilderness of Jeruel. But you will not even need to fight. Take your positions; then stand still and watch the Lord's victory. He is with you, O people of Judah and Jerusalem. Do not be afraid or discouraged. Go out against them tomorrow, for the Lord is with you!"* 2 Chronicles 20:15–17.

Imagine what those words meant to the whole nation: *you will not have to fight.* The battle belonged to the Lord. The confirmation comes by the mouth of the prophet, Jahaziel, son of Zechariah, son of Benaiah, son of Jeiel, son of Mattaniah, a Levite who was a descendant of Asaph. They are to stand still. This is what can happen when we fast and pray. The lesson here is that God responds to our worship.

He called for faith

Although the promise was received with joy, Jehoshaphat

still needed to encourage the people of God to have faith. Faith means acting on God's Word. They would still have to march out and form the battle lines. I love the words of King Jehoshaphat: *"Early the next morning the army of Judah went out into the wilderness of Tekoa. On the way Jehoshaphat stopped and said, 'Listen to me, all you people of Judah and Jerusalem! Believe in the Lord your God, and you will be able to stand firm. Believe in his prophets, and you will succeed"* 2 Chronicles 20:20.

Jehoshaphat appoints singers

Praise is a spiritual weapon. When we sing, the enemy gets confused. In this case, the enemy started killing each other when Jehoshaphat's singers opened their mouths to praise God. *"At the very moment they began to sing and give praise, the Lord caused the armies of Ammon, Moab, and Mount Seir to start fighting among themselves."* God's people obtained an unlikely victory. It all started with fasting and prayer. It continued in praise and ended in victory: *"Give thanks to the Lord; His faithful love endures forever"* 2 Chronicles 20:21.

Chapter Summary

At a time of great danger, the nation of Israel responded to the king's call. They fasted and prayed, worshipping and praising God. God responded to their plea and assured them of victory. God's people still needed to be encouraged in their faith. They had to act in faith, standing firm on the promises of God. On the battle line, each step forward was a step made in faith, trusting God to bring the promised redemption.

I can only imagine that morning when the Israelites woke up to the reality of their circumstances. They had to take their position, in the plain view of a ruthless enemy, who could destroy them in a matter of minutes. I can only imagine how their hearts conflicted between their unshakable faith in what God had said and the small but growing seeds of doubt. Like all of us, they could have easily asked themselves, what if …?

In times of great trial and difficulty, the people of God fasted and prayed. And God showed Himself to be faithful to His Word. Does that sound familiar?

Day Three

Personal Focus

Are you experiencing difficulty in your life? Maybe you are going through some troubled times in your marriage, finances or some relationship. Or maybe you know someone going through hardship. Have you found any encouragement in the Word of God today?

Use the space below to write down those encouragements and pray through each one of them.

Public Focus

Every church goes through times of difficulty. It could be some leadership crisis, illness, apathy, strained relationships, lack of adequate finances or lack of spiritual power. Share with your brothers and sisters, in a spirit of brokenness, the difficult time your church is going through.

Following your discussion, in love and honesty, write down these issues and pray for God to address each one of them.

Day Four
When God reveals His plan

Today's reading: Daniel 9.

There are times when God's Word speaks to us in a special way. It happens at the right time, in the right place, regarding a specific circumstance. I call these moments, 'times of revelation.' These are the times when God's Word comes alive in such a powerful way you feel your soul being lifted and nourished with hope!

We know Daniel as a mighty prophet and a man of faithfulness and integrity. We also remember Daniel for his prayer life (three times a day) and how God preserved him in the lion's den. Daniel was, indeed, a man of prayer. He must have been taken into exile to Babylon as a young man. While in exile, away from his family, relatives and any spiritual influence, Daniel maintained his relationship with God in prayer. Because of his stand, God gave him great favour and position in Babylon.

The key to Daniel's blessing and favour from God is found in Daniel 1:8, *"But Daniel was determined not to defile himself by eating the food and wine given to them by the king. He asked the chief of staff for permission not to eat these unacceptable foods."* When faced with the temptation to let go of his God, his values and his faith, Daniel decided in his heart that nothing in Babylon could match the joy of knowing God and being rightly related to Him. For Daniel, having God was the only way to succeed in a place like Babylon.

Warren Wiersbe suggests four principles that form the foundation of Daniel's success. I would like to expand on that framework because they are part and parcel of what made Daniel a man of God.

He believed in a sovereign God[3]

Daniel's life spanned the course of three empires: from the Babylonian Empire under Nebuchadnezzar through the Mede Empire under Darius and the Persian Empire under the rule of Cyrus. Daniel was a high official in all three empires. God used him in an elevated position at a time when Israel was but a faded memory. God had disciplined His people because of their disobedience and allowed King Nebuchadnezzar of Babylon to come and flatten Jerusalem and Israel's most beloved Temple. All through his life, Daniel (who was most likely in his late 80s by the time of this prayer), had no doubts about the sovereignty of God.

He had a disciplined prayer life

Daniel must have developed this habit of praying three times a day early in his life. In Daniel 2, King Nebuchadnezzar had a strange dream that he could not remember. The dream disturbed him so much he was willing to decapitate all the wise men of Babylon unless they communicated the dream and its meaning to him.

<u>When Daniel needed revelation, he prayed</u>. After Daniel spent time in prayer, the Lord revealed the dream and its meaning to him. *"Then Daniel went home and told his friends Hananiah, Mishael, and Azariah what had happened. He*

---
[3] Daniel 4:25, 32; 5:21.

urged them to ask the God of heaven to show them his mercy by telling them the secret, so they would not be executed along with the other wise men of Babylon. That night the secret was revealed to Daniel in a vision. Then Daniel praised the God of heaven" Daniel 2:17–19.

<u>When Daniel was threatened, he prayed</u>. Under Darius the Mede, it was the time when all the other officials became jealous of Daniel and tried to catch him doing something unlawful. Daniel was a man of full integrity, so they could not find any faults. They tricked the king into passing a law where no one was allowed to pray except to the king himself. As Daniel's character was impeccable, they tried to use his prayer life to discredit him before the king.

"Then the other administrators and high officers began searching for some fault in the way Daniel was handling government affairs, but they couldn't find anything to criticise or condemn. He was faithful, always responsible, and completely trustworthy. So they concluded, 'Our only chance of finding grounds for accusing Daniel will be in connection with the rules of his religion" Daniel 6:4–5. When Daniel heard of their plans, he went home and prayed to God, with his face towards Jerusalem, as if nothing had happened. In fact, when the officials came to arrest him at his house, they found him praying and asking God for help. God was about to answer his prayers. When Daniel was thrown into the den of lions, God kept their mouths shut. Daniel was spared while all the officials perished, along with their families.

He loved the Word of God and believed it

From his reading of Jeremiah, Daniel understood that God would allow 70 years of exile, followed by God's grace and mercy. God would bring His people back to Israel. Once Daniel understood that he began praying for the fulfilment of God's promise in His Word. Daniel was not prepared to sit and wait. He understood the call to prayer, and he obeyed immediately. Daniel was not satisfied with a passive attitude; he went into action. That action meant prayer. The more he prayed, the more convinced he was that God would keep His promise.

He had an understanding of spiritual warfare

In Daniel chapter ten, we find Daniel very aware of the reality of spiritual warfare. His prayer of intercession in chapter nine is followed by powerful visions of events concerning the future. The context of these visions is spiritual warfare. His reaction, again, was to fast and pray.

"When this vision came to me, I, Daniel, had been in mourning for three whole weeks. All that time I had eaten no rich food. No meat or wine crossed my lips, and I used no fragrant lotions until those three weeks had passed" Daniel 10:2–3.

Daniel's intercessory prayer, in chapter nine, follows God's revelation of the amazing plan to redeem Israel and bring them back from exile. Daniel began his prayer with confession and repentance. He confessed his own sins, as well as the sins of the nation.[4] He was broken over his own disobedience and that of the nation. He wept, and prayed.

---
[4] Daniel 9:20.

Chapter Summary

Daniel's prayer is full of passion and energy. If we want to learn to intercede for the nation, our church or ourselves, it is a good model to follow. There is nothing wrong with showing emotion in our prayer life. Emotions are very much part of how God created us to communicate. Imagine trying to share your love for your spouse without showing any emotion. Your communication will surely fail to achieve its desired goal.

The mighty prophet of God had the healthy habit of reading God's Word. In his reading, Daniel comes to understand that the 70 years of exile are about to come to an end. It must have been Daniel's calculation and his unshakable faith in God that motivated him to fast and pray right away.

"During the first year of his reign, I, Daniel, learned from reading the word of the Lord, as revealed to Jeremiah the prophet, that Jerusalem must lie desolate for seventy years. So I turned to the Lord God and pleaded with him in prayer and fasting. I also wore rough burlap and sprinkled myself with ashes" Daniel 9:2–3.

Daniel's prayer is what I refer to as an "O Lord" prayer. His prayer reflected the brokenness of his spirit and the deep desire of his heart. The "O Lord" type of prayers are filled with faith and desperation. In his prayer, Daniel focused on several things: the faithfulness of God, intercession for the nation and confession of sin (personal and national), identification with the historical sins of his fathers (the very sins that caused God to bring them into exile in Babylon), and the righteousness and holiness of God. Finally, Daniel concluded his prayer with an emphatic declaration: *"O Lord hear, O Lord forgive, O Lord listen, O Lord act."*

It is good to use this model of prayer to introduce intercession in the church prayer meetings. Intercessory prayer is not easy. It seems to be different from any other prayer. But the truth is we need intercessors today more than ever!

Day Four

Personal Focus

Has God spoken to you today through His Word? What did He say to you? Meditate on the times when God made His Word come alive for you. Maybe you've felt that God is silent for no reason at all. Pray for God's voice to speak again as you meditate on His Word.

Use the space below to write down the references or the things that God speaks, concerning your particular situation.

Public Focus

Paul encourages Timothy to give himself to the public reading of His Word. A healthy church is a church that honours God's Word above any other activity. A Bible centred church will be filled with the knowledge of God's will.

Take the time to read God's Word together and listen to His voice. Write down what you feel God is saying to you as a church from God's Word.

Day Five
God's challenge for spiritual revival

Today's reading: Joel chapters 1 and 2.

Barring a miracle, you cannot revive something that is already dead. But you can revive something that is barely alive. "Barely alive" is a term that could be used to describe the spiritual temperature of the Church in Western Europe. That is why we need reviving to a new and vibrant relationship with Jesus.

The prophecy of Joel comes as a response to imminent danger — a natural disaster in the form of a plague of locusts. A catastrophic drought would follow the plague.

Joel was a prophet during the early days of King Joash,[5] most likely when Jehoiada acted as a mentor and protector of the king. We are told that Joash became a king at the age of seven. It was customary for young kings to have an older official as mentor and protector.

King Joash is known for some amazing reforms and the spiritual revival of Israel. The revival in Joash's time could easily be linked to how Israel responded to the prophecy of Joel and God's call to fasting and prayer. The whole book of Joel centres on the theme of "the day of the Lord." This would be a day of judgment. Therefore, the people of God were called to prepare themselves.

Joel's interpretation of the three coming events is contained in his short prophecy. There would be three separate days

---
[5] 2 Kings 11-12.

of the Lord coming: the immediate, the imminent and the ultimate. The first would be the locusts, causing devastation and death. The second would be the Assyrians, who would come and conquer Judah. The ultimate day of the Lord would be the Final Judgment Day.

In the first event, the locusts seem to be a metaphorical army, bringing devastation and sorrow. In the second event, the locusts seem to be a real army, the Assyrians. They were well-known for their ruthless attitude in war. Such a conquest by the Assyrians could only be interpreted as God's judgment. In the third event, the locusts are not mentioned at all.

However, in spite of the fact that Joel's prophecy sounds dark and doom-laden, God gives great and powerful promises. God also uses Joel to challenge His people to a spiritual revival. He calls Judah to repent and turn away from sin. Part of that challenge is a call to fast and pray.

Before the day of judgment, the prophet Joel tells us, the Spirit of the Lord will be poured out on all flesh.[6] This promise was fulfilled on the day of Pentecost, when the Holy Spirit came upon the disciples gathered in the Upper Room.

On that day, the judgment will be poured out.[7] This is yet to happen. At the end of this age, when the earth and the heavens will pass away, every soul who has ever lived will be called before God to give an account for their lives.

After that day, blessing will be poured out as declared in Book of Joel.[8] This is the promise of a new creation where

---
6 Joel 2:28-32.
7 Joel 3:1-16.
8 Joel 3:17-21.

righteousness will dwell forever. There will be no more sin or suffering or pain. *"He will wipe every tear from their eyes, and there will be no more death or sorrow or crying or pain. All these things are gone forever"* Revelation 21:4.

As a prophetic book, Joel plays a significant role in the Word of God. Joel constitutes the foundation of the first public sermon in the Church age, delivered by Peter on the day of Pentecost.

Joel 2, although in the Old Testament, is a chapter about the Holy Spirit, just like Romans 8 in the New Testament. In both chapters, written centuries apart, we find the wonderful promise of the Holy Spirit, who comes to empower us to live a life worthy of God's name.

The promise, in Joel 2, begins with a proclamation: *"Sound the trumpet in Jerusalem. Raise the alarm on my holy mountain! Let everyone tremble in fear because the day of the Lord is upon us"* Joel 2:1. In the verses that follow, we are told how devastating this day of the Lord will be. There will be terror, people will be gripped by fear, and even the sun and the moon will go dark. This day of the Lord will be an awesome and terrible thing, and no one will escape it.

The proclamation is followed by a call to revival. *That is why the Lord says: "Turn to me now, while there is time. Give me your hearts. Come with fasting, weeping, and mourning. Don't tear your clothing in your grief, but tear your hearts instead"* Joel 2:12. Notice that God's call for revival includes fasting, weeping and mourning. The call continues in verse 15: *"Blow the ram's horn in Jerusalem! Announce a time of fasting; call the people together for a solemn meeting. Gather all the people — the elders, the children, and even the babies."*

The call to revival is followed by a promise of restoration. In verse 25, the Lord says, *"I will give you back what you lost to the swarming locusts, the hopping locusts, the stripping locusts, and the cutting locusts. It was I who sent this great destroying army against you."* Revival, as someone described it, is a new beginning of obedience to God. It is simply the beginning of God's restorative power at work in the Church. Everything that "the locusts" have eaten can and will be restored by God.

The promise of restoration is followed by the assurance of God's outpouring of His Holy Spirit, in verse 28: *"Then, after doing all those things, I will pour out my Spirit upon all people. Your sons and daughters will prophesy. Your old men will dream dreams, and your young men will see visions."*

Chapter Summary

In conclusion, revival is a day of a new beginning with God when the flickering ember bursts into flames, when sleeping Christians are infused with power and vitality, when the church learns to depend on God 100%, with total and sure abandonment to His will and purposes.

Here are some applications we can take from the book of Joel. God has promised to pour out His Holy Spirit. He has done that on the day of Pentecost. This promise also includes the fact that when the church answers God's call to repentance and returns to Him with fasting and prayer, the Lord is able to revive it.

God also promised that there would be signs in heaven and on earth. The book of Acts is filled with miracles and wonders, in heaven and on earth, which has proved God's Word repeatedly. The Apostles, following a threat from the Sanhedrin — the Religious Council of the Jews — prayed: *"Stretch out your hand with healing power; may miraculous signs and wonders be done through the name of your holy servant Jesus."* I find no Biblical reason not to pray today, just like they did. God has not changed at all. He is the same miracle worker as in the days of the Apostles.

God's promise in Joel 2 also includes the salvation of all those who call upon the name of the Lord. In every revival, there has been a natural consequence upon societies and communities. The revival of the Church will bring about the salvation of many souls.

As I said before, revival is the work of the Holy Spirit in the Church, turning the lukewarm Christian into a spiritually "highly flammable" follower of Jesus. The Holy Spirit can turn an indifferent Christian into a compassionate and loving person.

We understand that the Holy Spirit is here for this age of grace. We stand forgiven, and there is no more condemnation for those who are in Christ Jesus. Revival starts in the heart. It changes the spiritual atmosphere in the church and then, ultimately, it affects the community around us. Revival begins here, and it must begin on a personal level.

Day Five

Personal Focus

When was the last time you prayed for the revival of your own heart? Today, it's all about your relationship with the Holy Spirit. God's promise is for all of us. The fullness of His Holy Spirit is available to us all. However, the Holy Spirit (as a dove) is sensitive to sin and anything that can cause grievance to him.

Ask God to search your heart and reveal some of the things that need to be addressed. This is how personal revival begins.

Public Focus

The revival of God's Church begins with an attitude of humility as we seek God. Then, God revives those who come to him in honesty and acknowledge their desperate need of Him.

Does your church need revival? Can you take time, as a church, to ask God for a spiritual revival? Fasting and prayer is a way to show God you are serious about it.

Day Six
Waiting for a promise to be fulfilled

Today's reading: Luke 2:25–40.

It appears that most of us are not good at waiting. However, there are times when we have no choice but to wait. Despite our wanting to see everything done "yesterday", God has His own timing.

The period between the two Testaments is a period of waiting. The blank page in your Bibles, found between the two Testaments, covers 400 years of history. During this period, God appears to be silent.

God's last words in the Old Testament were given to the prophet Malachi. The prophet Malachi finished his prophecy, just like Joel, speaking about the coming "day of the Lord." However, his prophecy ended with the promise of the great prophet Elijah, who would prepare the way for the Messiah. *"Look, I am sending you the prophet Elijah before the great and dreadful day of the Lord arrives. His preaching will turn the hearts of fathers to their children, and the hearts of children to their fathers. Otherwise I will come and strike the land with a curse"* Malachi 4:5–6.

During the 400 years of 'silence', the people of God had seen their hopes of freedom slowly dying, as several rebellions against the Roman occupation were brutally suppressed. Their political leaders had failed to lead a successful revolt against their oppressors and restore the throne of King David.

Many Jews believed that their moral and religious values had been lost. Some had retreated into the wilderness, living in closed communities, trying to save their faith in God by physical means. Others had taken the law into their own hands. Three generations of revolutionaries had tried to fulfil the Messianic expectations, with no success. Many great military leaders, among them the Maccabees, had been caught and killed by the Romans.

Although people still believed in the promise of God for a Messiah and Saviour, most of them had become tired of waiting and had given up! However, a small group continued to believe. They had not given up! Waiting is not easy, but we are encouraged to persevere and wait patiently on the Lord, who keeps all His promises.

"Wait patiently for the Lord. Be brave and courageous. Yes, wait patiently for the Lord" Psalm 27:14.

"Such things were written in the Scriptures long ago to teach us. And the Scriptures give us hope and encouragement as we wait patiently for God's promises to be fulfilled" Romans 15:4.

The good news is that we have, in the Bible, enough examples of people who have patiently waited for God's promises to be fulfilled. They did it with fasting and prayer. Two such wonderful saints were Simeon and Anna.

Simeon
We are not told much about Simeon. We do not know anything about his background, his occupation, or any details surrounding his family. The details we are given

concern his character, his waiting, his relationship with the Holy Spirit, and how he held on to God's promise for the Messiah.

"At that time there was a man in Jerusalem named Simeon. He was righteous and devout and was eagerly waiting for the Messiah to come and rescue Israel. The Holy Spirit was upon him and had revealed to him that he would not die until he had seen the Lord's Messiah" Luke 2:25–26.

Simeon's righteousness and devotion to God must have been so visible to those around him that the writer of the Gospel, Luke the doctor, does not seem to feel the need to give any extra explanation. He was simply "a righteous man." Everyone could see it, so Luke states that fact with ease. It fascinates me to consider that Simeon, a righteous man, is in Jerusalem at that exact time when Jesus is brought to the Temple to be circumcised. You and I should know that these details are not simple coincidences.

We are also told that Simeon was eagerly waiting for the Messiah to come and rescue Israel. What is amazing is that, unlike his contemporaries, Simeon was able to recognise God's Messiah in baby Jesus. This little detail caused many to stumble and miss the coming of the Messiah altogether. Simeon must have spent his entire life waiting. Eugene Peterson describes Simeon using a wonderful choice of words: *"a good man, a man who lived in the prayerful expectancy of help for Israel"* Luke 2:25–32 The Message Bible. Another important aspect regarding Simeon is: *"The Holy Spirit was upon him."* This clearly indicates that Simeon was set apart by God for a specific purpose. In Joel 2, we have seen how prayer and fasting can result in a filling with the Holy Spirit. Simeon's prayerful expectation of God to rescue Israel produced a man filled with the Holy Spirit.

It is the Holy Spirit who revealed to Simeon that he would not die until he saw the salvation of the Lord. The grammar of the text suggests that the promise had been made sometime in the distant past. However, on that specific day, it was also the Holy Spirit who led him into the Temple. Here is a righteous man, led by the Holy Spirit, having an attitude of waiting while praying.

That day, his waiting came to an end. All his prayers were finally answered. His joy was so full and complete that Simeon declared his readiness to be released from this life; what an amazing way to live and die!

Anna
Anna was a prophetess, and her story is very similar to that of Simeon. We are given a few more details about Anna. We know she was from the tribe of Asher, the daughter of Phanuel. The tribe of Asher inherited the region of Galilee, so we can assume she had lived away from home for most of her life.

We also know that she was a widow, most likely around 84 years old. She had been married to her husband for seven short years, and after his death, she came to live at the Temple. The next detail is as fascinating as it is to be admired: *"She never left the Temple but stayed there day and night, worshipping God with fasting and prayer"* Luke 2:37. Anna worshipped the Lord, night and day, with fasting and prayer. The fact that she was there on that very same day, alongside Simeon, suggests that God had placed them there for the same reason: to meet Jesus. It is very probable that both had the same prayerful expectation: the coming of God's Messiah. God, being faithful to His promises, blessed them both with a personal preview of His salvation.

"She came along just as Simeon was talking with Mary and Joseph, and she began praising God. She talked about the child to everyone who had been waiting expectantly for God to rescue Jerusalem" Luke 2:38.

Anna does not seem to stop at praising God for the awesome privilege of seeing Jesus, the promised Messiah and the salvation of God. She goes on to tell everyone about the baby — to all whose hearts were filled with expectation. For them, the waiting had ended. Waiting was replaced by exuberant joy and peace. The promise had been fulfilled; no more waiting.

Chapter Summary

Waiting can turn into frustration and disappointment. Do not give up! Persevere with fasting and prayer. Worship the Lord as you wait. Salvation will come, but expect to be surprised. Sometimes, God answers in ways we do not expect. Everyone expected a Messiah, but not many expected a baby. Simeon and Anna, as much as the shepherds and the wise men, accepted that the answer had finally come in the way of a baby.

Part 3 – Start the journey

God has made some wonderful and amazing promises in His Word. Many have been fulfilled throughout history; others are yet to be fulfilled. God is in the business of keeping his Word, *"For all of God's promises have been fulfilled in Christ with a resounding 'Yes!' And through Christ, our 'Amen' (which means 'Yes') ascends to God for his glory"* 2 Corinthians 1:20.

Day Six

Personal Focus

Has God given you any personal promises through His Word? What are the things you are waiting for? As you fast and pray, take time to bring your needs and struggles to God. See if there are any promises for you in God's Word.

Write down these promises and bring them to God again, with a renewed commitment to wait for their fulfilment.

Public Focus

God's promises are amazing, and He will keep them no matter how long we must wait. If God has given you as a church, precious promises, do not give up while you wait. Do not lose hope. Trust in His Word.

Use the space below to write down these precious promises and continue to pray, as a church, for their fulfilment. Or maybe you need to write down new promises God has given you as you pray. Listen to God's voice and remember His faithfulness.

Day Seven
Fasting and Prayer in times of ministry

Reading: Acts 13:1–3; 14:21–28.

Church leaders are expected to make informed and wise decisions. Among other decisions, they have to identify new leaders, train and release them into the ministry. Then there are issues of discipline and discipleship in the churches. How do we know we are making the right decisions?

Let's look at Jesus and see how He made decisions. We should start by looking back at the beginning of the Gospels when Jesus is about to start His earthly ministry. Try to imagine the moment, and understand its significance.

The Son of God is about to announce to the world that God's Kingdom has arrived. Jesus is about to call everybody to repentance. Jesus is about to invite the men and women of His own country, and in time the whole world, to believe in Him and His Good News. God's plan of salvation is about to be revealed to the whole world. Jesus is about to announce that He is the Messiah, the Son of God.

The implications of His ministry are going to be cosmic. People on earth will learn that salvation is by faith in Him alone. The demons and the devil himself are about to go into a frenzy, trying to interfere and stop Him. The whole of heaven, the angels, and Moses and Elijah, will testify to this ministry in one way or another.

Part 3 – Start the journey

Following His baptism, the Word of God tells us in Matthew 4:1, Jesus was led by the Spirit into the wilderness, where He fasted and prayed for forty days and nights. During this time, His earthly body must have become weak and vulnerable. We see the devil trying to use such a moment of physical weakness to tempt Him with food, power and influence. Each time, Jesus used the Word of God to resist those temptations. He came out of that time of fasting and prayer *"filled with the Holy Spirit's power"* Luke 4:14.

I believe Jesus was fully God. He never ceased to be God at any point in His earthly ministry. I also believe He was fully man; as John says, *"the Word became human and made his home among us. He was full of unfailing love and faithfulness. And we have seen his glory, the glory of the Father's one and only Son"* John 1:14. But I also believe the purpose of His time in the wilderness, His fasting and prayer, was to teach us that ministry must be in the power of the Holy Spirit.

The same is true for the Apostles. In Acts 11:9, we read about the disciples who had been scattered because of persecution. Some of them travelled as far as Phoenicia, Cyprus and Antioch of Syria. Some believers from Cyprus and Cyrene[9] preached the Good News to the Gentiles of Antioch, and a vibrant church was quickly formed.

Barnabas was then sent by the church in Jerusalem to confirm the news coming from Antioch of Syria. Upon arrival, Barnabas saw the evidence of God's grace and power clearly manifested in the church.

---

9 On the north coast of Africa.

Paul, who had been recently converted through the ministry of the Holy Spirit, is also added to the ministry team. This was the beginning of a fantastic missionary initiative that brought the gospel our way. We should never forget that we received the gospel because a group of believers in Syria listened to the Holy Spirit and acted in obedience.

In Acts 13, we find the church in Antioch on the verge of a great missionary campaign. The gospel was about to reach Europe.

The ministry team

The priority of every new ministry should be the formation of a team. In Acts 13, the church in Antioch had a team formed by the Holy Spirit, filled with diversity. Notice the diverse personalities and backgrounds.

Barnabas was known for being gentle. Simeon seemed to have been from Niger, most likely an African. Lucius was most likely a Greek from Cyrene, eastern Lybia, in North Africa. Manaen spent his childhood in the presence of King Herod Antipas. Paul (formerly Saul) was a Jew of excellent spiritual pedigree, a firebrand filled with passion. The collective strength of the team was remarkable. The main spiritual gifts of the team were teaching and prophecy. Their common activity was worship. They were actively worshipping God with fasting and prayer.

The team listened to the Holy Spirit

While they worshipped the Lord, with fasting and prayer, they became sensitive to the voice of the Holy Spirit. This is very important. Please note that worship is not just about praying and praising God, but also about listening. If we do not take time to listen, we might miss what the Lord wants to say.

"One day as these men were worshipping the Lord and fasting, the Holy Spirit said, 'Appoint Barnabas and Saul for the special work to which I have called them.' So after more fasting and prayer, the men laid their hands on them and sent them on their way" Acts 13:2–3.

Notice how the whole team heard the voice of the Holy Spirit. He made it clear to all of them that Barnabas and Saul were to be set aside for a special work.

The team released a team

God places His people in community. When God called Moses, He also called Aaron. Joshua had Caleb. David had Jonathan. Jesus sent His disciples, two by two, with power and authority. God does that because this is how He works. There is community in the Godhead. The Father created through the Word (the Eternal Son) by the Holy Spirit. If God exists and works in community, so should we.

Working with others is not always easy. But we must make every effort to let God shape us into team members.

Not everyone can be a leader, but everyone can be a team member. One significant aspect of working in a team is a growing sensitivity to the Holy Spirit and hearing and together confirming what God is saying.

Fast forward a bit, and we get to the end of this amazing mission trip in Acts 14. After travelling to Cyprus and preaching the gospel to the governor of the Island in Paphos, Paul and Barnabas travelled to Perga. From Perga, they went to Antioch of Pisidia. God moves among the Jews and Gentiles of Pisidia, with many coming to Christ, but the opposition forced Paul and Barnabas to flee. They went to Iconium, where the same thing happened. When the mob forced them to leave, Paul and Barnabas went to Lystra and Derbe in the region of Lycaonia. Wherever they went, they preached the Good News, and many people were converted. During their stay in Lystra, a crippled man was healed. The crowd went ecstatic and began to worship the Apostles as gods. This broke their heart, but both saw this as an opportunity to point the people to Jesus.

As they visited the churches formed during their travel, Paul and Barnabas appointed teams of elders. Teams multiply teams. Leaders multiply leaders. The appointment of elders was made with fasting and prayer. *"Paul and Barnabas also appointed elders in every church. With prayer and fasting, they turned the elders over to the care of the Lord, in whom they had put their trust"* Acts 14:23.

Chapter Summary

As we wrap up this chapter, we find a clear lesson here. Fasting and prayer is the best environment for making God-glorifying decisions. It is in the context of worship that we can allow space for the Holy Spirit to speak. Fasting and prayer is the best practice to use in appointing leaders. Then we can leave them in the care of the Holy Spirit.

Every church is faced with new challenges. Every church is meant to go on and continue the mission: sharing the gospel, making disciples, raising leaders and planting other churches. Taking the time to fast and pray may save us a lot of pain later. Having the wrong person released into a ministry, or the wrong person appointed to a leadership position without the approval of the Holy Spirit, can cause a lot of pain in the church and even cause division. Jesus and His Apostles teach us that ministry, carried out in the power of the Holy Spirit, begins and is sustained by fasting and prayer. I hope we can learn from them and avoid the pain of making wrong decisions.

Day Seven

Personal Focus

Set some time aside to reflect on the words of today's reading. It could be that you are facing a crossroads. To some, this may be the end of the road. To others, it may be the beginning of a new path. Take time to ask God for wisdom in making the right decision.

Write down the decisions that you are asked to make. Pray over each one of them, and let God give you insight and wisdom to do the God-honouring thing.

Public Focus

Churches often face critical times such as making important decisions. It could be the call of a new pastor. It could be the start of a building project, a new church plant, or simply a small change that could cause division.

Use the space below to write down those challenges and pray in unity for God's wisdom. God gives wisdom to those who ask. Fast and pray for the way forward.

Part 4

Moving on

What's next?

Since the empowering of the Church on the day of Pentecost, the disciples have followed the example of Jesus in their approach to ministry. Pray in the upper room, then go to the marketplace.

I hope you have been blessed by reading this book. My prayer, while writing it, has been that you, the individual follower of Jesus, and the Church will discover or rediscover the joy and the power of fasting and prayer. I continue to pray that as you uncover the treasure of God's Word on this subject, you will develop the practice of fasting and praying. Whether it will be on your own, as a couple or family, with a small group or the whole church, it is important you do not settle for an intellectual understanding of this subject. Put into practice everything you have learnt and make it a discipline.

The disciples were commanded to wait in Jerusalem until they received the gift of the Holy Spirit. He would empower them to be witnesses of Jesus, His life, His death, His resurrection and His teachings. They were to start in Jerusalem, then in Judea, Samaria and to the ends of the earth. The disciples were commanded to go into the whole world to make disciples of all nations. This is the Great Commission which, we all accept, applies to every disciple of Jesus, men and women, young and old.

But what is the next step in fulfilling this Great Commission? How do we move on from here? Some have emphasised "the waiting" to the extent that they have never got around to "the going." Some have been excited about going, but neglected the waiting, and have rushed into the marketplace without the power of the Holy Spirit.

The book of Acts sheds some light on this issue. The disciples waited for ten days. They prayed and most likely fasted. On the day of Pentecost, those who gathered in the Upper Room were filled with the Holy Spirit. They could have spent the whole day in that amazing ecstasy, praising God and having some wonderful fellowship. But no, they immediately went into the marketplace, renewed and filled with power, sharing the Good News of Jesus. That day, 3,000 souls were added to the Church.

Once opposition arose, they went back to the Upper Room. They prayed, were filled again with the Holy Spirit, and went back into the marketplace. The book of Acts is filled with the constant repetition of this simple but powerful sequence: the Upper Room, then the marketplace, back to the Upper Room and then back into the marketplace.

If we miss one step, we get "out of sync" and end up outside the intended pattern of the Church. Stick with the sequence: Upper Room, marketplace, and repeat!

Appendix 1

A life of prayer and power

This book is meant to motivate you to a continuous life of fasting and prayer. Your journey of seven days was filled with purpose, but life continues, and fasting and prayer must become your lifestyle as a Christian. A life of fasting and prayer means a life of power.

Let me give you an example:

My father came to Christ during communism, from a life of sin and violence. After a dramatic and miraculous conversion, the elders of the small church he was attending, approached him and said: "We see in you the spiritual gifts of a leader, and we want you to join us for some training." For most of us, this would mean some sort of theological training. But no, that was not their plan.

How would you "train" a young man who clearly displayed spiritual gifts for leadership? "Meet us on top of the hill which overlooks the town," they said to my father. "We'll meet there every morning at 6.00 am, before going to work. We are going to pray."

This was their strategy and training method: if you want to lead, you must learn to pray. If you want to preach, you must learn to pray. This reminds me of the Apostles. Jesus was about to entrust the Church to the Apostles, and there was no Church manual, no seminar for preaching and no Bible colleges.

Now, don't get me wrong. All these things are good and useful. They play a part in our formation, but we must put first things first.

The Apostles asked: *"Lord, teach us to pray!"* Luke 11:1. Somehow, the Apostles connected the dots: John the Baptist prayed. His disciples prayed. Jesus prayed. He often went away early in the morning, sometimes all night. All He did was pray to the Father. Then, He came down among all the people, meeting their needs, healing the sick and delivering them out of bondage. He preached, but not like the Pharisees. He spoke with power and performed mighty miracles.

I'm pretty certain they concluded that prayer had something to do with it all. The disciples must have understood a vital truth, which I believe we have lost today: Prayer means power, and power changes the way we do things. *Do you see it?*

Those elders, who are now with the Lord, understood this truth so well. Because of them, my father's life and ministry have been marked by prayer. It's been all about private and public prayer.

Appendix 1

My father often prayed on his own, with tears and passion. We, his seven children, witnessed this regularly. He never had much theological training, but he witnessed the power of God through the most difficult period of Church history in Romania: communism. The prayer meetings lasted for a few hours, with everyone on their knees, crying out to God with sincere tears.

Things are not the same today, mostly because we have lost this connection between prayer, power and preaching. Our theology and thirst for intellectual knowledge, has replaced our passion for praise and intimacy with God.

That is why we must learn again to stay close to God and guard our prayer life. Learn to pray, and you will have power to preach. Seek to be in the prayer meeting, and you will love the church. Pray, and the Holy Spirit will reveal to you the truth of His Word. Pray and you will have wisdom and understanding.

Prayer also equips you to do the work of an evangelist. It is only in prayer that you become more and more burdened for lost souls. If you want to see a united church, then get the church to pray.

I must say, this challenges the way we view training for preaching and ministry. I know people who have fallen in love with the pulpit, but not in love with God.

Have a look at the book of Acts. It was in a prayer meeting of 120 disciples that the Holy Spirit came and baptised the church with power. Then the early Church went forward, on their knees. Every time the world, sin or opposition tried to destroy it, the Church had victory because of prayer. Yes, there was suffering. Yes, some of them died. But the church had power. Throughout the book of Acts, churches are planted, and disciples receive the Holy Spirit during prayer times.

Prayer, power and preaching are all connected. This demands our response. It's quite simple: if you desire the pulpit or to lead the church, learn to pray.

Note: This article is part of the Preacher's Hub, the preaching training group, in Transformation Centre, Lisburn. For similar articles, go to our website: www.transformation.cc

Appendix 2

Fasting and Prayer with John Wesley

John Wesley (17 June 1703 – 2 March 1791), the founder of Methodism, encouraged the members of his societies to fast on both Wednesdays and Fridays as a regular spiritual discipline.

John Wesley would not ordain anyone into the ministry if they were unwilling to fast on the given days. Towards the end of his ministry, however, Wesley settled for the normal Anglican tradition of fasting just on Fridays.

In fact, John Wesley advocated fasting on Fridays as early as 1739. His fast would start on Thursday night at sundown. This seems to coincide with the Jewish tradition of considering sundown the start of a new day. Wesley would end the fast on Friday around 3.00 pm.

The Methodist Revival and the church-planting movement began with a few men gathering together to pray, fast, read the Bible and encourage each other to holy living. This "holy club" formed at Oxford University (the 1720s), which included John and Charles Wesley, was the foundation for what later became Methodist societies.

As the doors of the Anglican churches began to close, John Wesley began preaching to the crowds in the open fields around Bristol. This new way of preaching spread quickly, and John Wesley travelled the country, establishing societies of people willing to gather, based on the same principles of the "holy club." Throughout his life, Wesley spent an incredible amount of time organising these societies on Biblical principles. His attention to careful methods for studying the Word of God, praying and exercising spiritual disciplines such as fasting, gave the movement the name of "Methodist." The encouragement to fast, as a regular spiritual discipline, is as effective as developing the discipline of reading God's Word and praying.

I have found Wesley's principles for fasting quite helpful and filled with common sense. I have copied them from the Methodist prayer website. For more details visit: www.methodistprayer.org

What I have tried to explain in my own words, John Wesley seems to be able to put in a well-prepared and concise list. Of course, lists are not everyone's thing. However, they can be useful guidelines and reminders of what we can do to refocus on what is important.

Lists can be beneficial for those who have busy lives and just want to get a glimpse of what needs to be considered as they fast and pray.

The following list is based on the words of John Wesley (I am confident he never said you might want to switch things up — No 18th century Englishman had that phrase in his vocabulary!)

The Wesley Fast

1. Be flexible and listen to the Holy Spirit. Don't get so caught up with the act of fasting itself that you forget why you're doing it in the first place.

2. Decide whether you're going to do a complete fast (water only), a no-solid-food fast that allows milk, juice, coffee and tea, a no-meat fast, or some other kind of fast. There are no fixed rules here, but it's always good to try to keep the fast you set out to do. Some fasts are more difficult than others, and there will be times you may feel led to switch things up.

3. Plan on Friday as your regular fasting day, but use Wednesday and other days for additional fasting when you feel called to a time of deeper and more intense prayer. Remember, there's nothing "magic" about Friday. It's simply a historical day for fasting in many Christian traditions, largely because Jesus was crucified on a Friday. If for some reason another day of the week makes more sense for you, then fast on that day.

4. Only fast for more than one consecutive day after you've consulted with your doctor and only if you're sure you're physically able to handle it.

5. Make sure you drink plenty of water while fasting, no matter what kind of fast you choose.

6. *The default Wesley Fast is observed from sundown Thursday till 3:00 Friday afternoon. Some Christians go till sundown on Friday. Do whichever you feel led to do in any given week.*

7. *Remember, there will be times when it makes sense to skip your Friday fast or move it to another day of the week. For example, if you have an opportunity to have lunch on a Friday with someone you've been wanting to connect with for a while, don't feel compelled to create an awkward situation by sticking to your fast. Just change your fast day that week. Guideline #1 applies here.*

CONTACT DETAILS
Pastor Nick Serb
Transformation Centre
137 Gregg Street, Lisburn
Northern Ireland
Charity No: NIC - 106628

E: info@transformation.cc
T: +44 (0) 28 92665647
W: www.transformation.cc

Inspired to write a book?

Contact

Maurice Wylie Media

Your Inspirational Christian Publisher

Based in Northern Ireland and distributing around the world

www.MauriceWylieMedia.com

Maurice Wylie Media
Receive 5% off your
next book order by
using this coupon code
* THANKINGYOU *